Water Over Time

A Collection of Stories and Poems

Barbara Toboni

MoonSkye Publishing
Napa, California
www.moonskyepublishing.com

Copyright © 2013 by Barbara Toboni

The stories and poems in this collection were inspired by my life in Guam with some changes to names and situations in order to enhance real-life events.

All rights are reserved including the right to reproduce this book or portions thereof except for brief quotations used in reviews.

ISBN-10: 0984863656
ISBN-13: 978-0-9848636-5-5

Cover painting copyright © 2013 by Elaine Lewis.

All pictures of the author as a young girl were taken by Morton Friedman, Barbara's father.

MoonSkye Publishing
151 2nd St., #5562
Napa, CA 94581

To David
who journeyed to Guam with me.

Table of Contents

Water Over Time 1

A Deal with Dad 2

Cave Girl 5

The Beach Saved Me 6

Culture Shock 7

Authority: What was Dad Thinking? 8

Frog 10

Geckos vs. Cockroaches 11

Island Girl 16

The Experiment 18

The Zori Sisters 20

JR's Party 23

Frankenstein's Motel 25

Mother of Me 27

A Party in Agat 28

He Taught Me How 30

Acknowledgements 31

About the Author 32

WATER OVER TIME

All I know now
is what I remember

Forty years
have swallowed
my house

Mold on concrete
is hard to remove
easier to build anew

In the mom and pop
across the street
I bought cigarettes
for 35 cents

A proud clerk
tells me this was
the first store
in Talofofo

Too young
for cigarettes
too old for
lollipops

I peer
through bamboo reeds
afraid to go inside

Water over time
is sacred

A Deal with Dad

I told Dad he could take me to Guam if he bought me a horse. I'd always wanted to own a horse, wished for one on every birthday candle since I was old enough to swing my leg over a saddle. Unfortunately, our family never lived on property large enough to accommodate a horse, and after countless conversations with my father about the cost and the chores of ownership, I stopped asking for one of my own. Instead, I settled for visits to a stable nearby and their much too short trail rides.

Searching for a reason to look forward to our Guam move, I struck a deal with Dad. "Buy me a horse and I'll go."

Not wanting to disappoint his youngest daughter, Dad said, "I'll do my best to find you a horse."

On a flat-topped hillside in the nearby village of Talofofo, he located a working ranch with stables for six horses. The owners, a family of five, lived in both a trailer and a cave. The cave served as a storm shelter to protect the family. In 1967, the year before our family moved to Guam, Typhoon Karen pummeled the island. We were warned by residents that super storms like Karen occurred about once per decade, and although concrete was used in the construction of newer homes like ours in Ipan, this family had seen enough destruction to have an emergency plan. Why not make use of the cave located on the property?

My first island summer the family invited me to work with them and take care of their beautiful horses. I helped on trail rides, and spent time with the girls, Meling, my own age, and Lani, her older sister. We all became friends and I soon discovered they shared a cave bedroom. Little brother, Johnny slept in the trailer with his parents.

The front of the cave cut into volcanic cliff facing the east side of the island overlooking the bay. To get inside we walked a narrow pathway along the edge of the property. The first and largest room of the two-room dwelling, a kitchen, was protected at the entrance by a separate rock wall, which stood alone like a giant door without hinges.

To the right of the kitchen, the bedroom was smaller, but with an opening like an enormous mouth yawning over the valley and Talofofo Bay below. Imagine a skyscraper view, but from a cave. A real estate ad might read: natural volcanic construction, open sky lighting, ocean air, cool year-round. Extra amenities: durable stick-like furnishings, appliances, and a working kitchen sink. Outhouse located elsewhere on premises.

This deal with Dad, although a variation of our original agreement, satisfied me. I went from a pestering little princess back to the more polite variety everyone could stand to be around. Dad, I am pleased to say, kept his side of our bargain.

Cave Girl

I rode horses with Meling
she slept in a cave
overlooking Talofofo Bay
safe from typhoons

Cave girl's ancestors
freak out
a fire pit modernized
maze of pipes, hoses
strapped to ceilings

Peculiar cousins
senseless chores
spraying dirt floors
sprinkle sweep
sprinkle sweep
to keep dust down

And me, who am I
sitting high
atop the railed bed
swinging legs
to sounds from a box

On rock walls stick shadows dance
Gary Puckett and the Union Gap
"Young Girl"

The Beach Saved Me

Behind our house
a sandy little path
led to the beach

I'd lose myself
on sunny afternoons
collect bits of coral
shells and driftwood

Swim and slosh around
in old tennis shoes
make footprints

Write notes and prayers
in the sand
DEAR GOD
GET ME OFF THIS ISLAND

The beach
is what saved me

Culture Shock

What do you expect
a teen to do
with no phone
no TV remote

Idle hands
smoke cigarettes

I look cool
at Talofofo Bay
learn to body surf
in warm brown waves

Sticky black sand
fills my suit

Authority: What was Dad Thinking?

My father, an authority on most things, got the education thing wrong when we moved to Guam. After speaking to other authorities on the subject, he decided the Catholic school curriculum was more advanced, therefore better than the public schools. He enrolled my older sister and me in Catholic school. We failed miserably. My science teacher, a nun from Korea, talked so fast that spit ejected from her mouth, and her scribbles on the board were confusing and useless to me.

It wasn't only our grades that suffered. Our behavior took a bad spin too. Seemed everywhere we turned we were breaking some rule or another, skirt lengths, bubble gum, make-up, the wrong kind of scarf or headband, and once my sister had a note sent home; holding hands with her boyfriend in the hallways. I saw a lot worse things going on in the hallways, but I think those nuns had it in for us, the Jewish sisters.

Jewish girls in a parochial school? What was Dad thinking?

Every infraction of the code carried a fine, a dollar for chewing gum, or for skirts rolled up. The note home for the boyfriend was probably the last straw. After a few short months my Dad had had enough. Between the lousy grades and the fines he yanked us out of there and plopped us in public school where we behaved like angels or no one seemed to notice us.

Public school had a few challenges of its own. We picked up the nasty habit of cigarette smoking so we could fit in, but we steered clear of anything dangerous like getting involved in the fights between rival gangs of Guamanians and Filipinos. Once, when a girl in the bathroom demanded a cigarette and I didn't have one she threatened to beat me up. Luckily the bell rang. I always carried extra cigarettes after that.

With improved grades and no fines, Dad was happy and could go back to being the authority figure I loved and respected.

Frog

My first date
the boy I kissed
nearly sucked
my tongue
out of my mouth

At first I thought
he's a nice boy
a beautiful
Guamanian boy
why would he do
something like that

We both attended
Catholic school
Did that
have something
to do with it

GECKOS VS. COCKROACHES

Guam's geckos ate bugs of all kinds: spiders, crickets, moths, and mosquitoes. Those darling, pale brown lizards were my heroes. I didn't scream when I saw them sticking to the ceiling or scrambling from a drawer.

But I shrieked at cockroaches. Those spastic and nasty, greasy and foul, monsters of the insect world seemed to head right towards me when I flipped the light switch.

Island paradise
    fever
Everyone familiar
    gossip
Damp air, fewer wrinkles
    hair frizzles
Suntan   overdone
    sunburn
Village fiestas
    flies
Tropic breezes
    storms
Ocean views
    tourists
Geckos   snack on
    cockroaches

First Guam neighborhood.

Neighborhood store.

Ready to ride in the Liberation Day Parade, 1968.

Mellow and me, 1971.

JR's band, 1975. JR is 4th from the left.

Author's sister, Nancy, at 16.

Island Girl

Whatever happened
to that picture
me 16 or so
sitting cross-legged
outside the tent
naked to the waist

A group of us pretended
we were natives
camped out
at Cocos Island
sailed there by boat

We skinny-dipped
our pale skin
pearled
luminous
in moonlight

Whatever happened
to that picture
me frizzy-haired
dreamy-eyed
virginesque

Years later
I found out
you showed

that picture
to everyone

Hey
where is that picture
it's proof
I'm an island girl

The Experiment

It's not like anyone twisted my arm
I knew what I was doing

A group of us did it together
in my living room
after an hour or so
we became zombies

Slack-bodied
and strewn around the room
on couches and chairs

That's all I remember

But I am told there were
hallucinations
that I pretended
to be smoking cigarettes

Tried to arrange my body
so that I sat
legs dangling up
instead of down

At the hospital
a doctor pumped my stomach
shot me full of downers
my father watched
his face drained of color

Later I was told the medicine
I injested was 5 capsules
of belladonna

I slept it off
apologized to my parents
about a thousand times

A month or two later
I dropped a tab of LSD
guess I wasn't done
experimenting

The Zori Sisters

At seventeen, I graduated high school, my older sister moved out, and my best friend left the island. Concerned that I would be lonely, my parents bought me a puppy, a beagle I named Mellow. I loved owning a dog and enjoyed our long walks together. On one of these walks I met Sunny.

"How adorable!" Sunny knelt to pet Mellow, a smile blooming from the point of her chin to the tip of her nose.

"Thanks. I'm trying to teach him to walk with a leash."

"Cool. You live around here?" The pup leaned against Sunny's leg, a paw catching on one of her rubber shoes.

"The end of the street. Wanna walk with us?" Maybe she had other plans, but I hoped not, because I wanted the company and she liked my dog. I tugged Mellow off her foot and noticed our sandals matched, same color, bright orange.

Sunny gathered long strands of her unruly hair and twisted it all into a bun. She pointed to our flip-flops. "Look at us, The Zori Sisters."

Matching sandals, wild hair, we could have been related. Delighted to find a new friend, Sunny filled my sister gap as we flip-flopped all over Apra Heights, the Quonset hut Theater, Navy Mini Mart, and the neighborhood park.

I told her all about myself, and vice versa only her versa was immensely different than mine. Only two years my senior, she had been married, given birth to a stillborn baby, and her marriage was annulled. Wow! In a short expanse of time Sunny had lived, really lived, and I wanted to know all the details, but shied away from asking. Our friendship was too new, and nosey wasn't my style.

Sunny's name matched her personality, and her cheerful chatter saved me from my lonely condition. I had begun writing poetry, depressing stuff with lines like, "Love dies as machines blacken the world." Breaking my own privacy rule, I allowed my new friend to see my writing. She said my poems were sensitive and honest. She would know because her mother also wrote poetry.

Gradually, Sunny confided in me about her ex mother-in-law, saying the woman had demanded an end to her marriage. She blamed the girl for cursing her own pregnancy and causing the child's stillbirth. I couldn't imagine such cruelty, but my friend told me the woman didn't approve of her, a white girl marrying her Guamanian son.

Sunny said the woman taught her to cook. One dish, chop steak, I liked so much she shared the recipe. "Be careful of the curse," she warned.

"Really? How silly." I didn't believe her.

Because my own mother taught me, "The way to a man's heart is through his stomach," I served the dish to Kenny, the boy next door, my secret crush. It worked. Kenny raved about the meal, and he proceeded to get me drunk on a bottle of wine he had acquired somewhere. We went for a walk after dinner, and I carelessly left the empty bottle on the kitchen table. When I returned home Dad lectured me about having boys in the house without parental supervision and underage drinking.

The more I stir-fried steak, the more it seemed Sunny's warning had merit, more stubbed toes and sidewalk stumbles, rainy days and lost umbrellas, and the final row that broke it off with Kenny.

A few years later, when I married JR, I changed the recipe by adding garlic, ginger, and sesame oil. I renamed the dish Sunny's Stir-fry Steak. Would my luck change too? JR loved it, and ate it all the time—until the divorce.

JR'S PARTY

Anyone wanna go
to a party
at the golf course?

Gonna be wild, man

Whose party?

JR

JR?

Yeah, you know
JR and his band

You mean the band
from the teen club?

Yeah, gonna be wild
Everybody will be there

Everybody?

JR knows everybody
Like the whole island

I don't really know him
Danced with him once
Sort of
From the stage
He watched me
Cute guy

So, wanna go?

Sure
Hope he remembers
Me

FRANKENSTEIN'S MOTEL

After high school
my parents
announced plans
for a divorce
As remedy
I moved into
Frank and Stephen's Motel

My sister and her boyfriend
managed the place
They needed a maid
I wanted a room
Free rent for work
I did not know
the word work

I scrubbed floors
bleached toilets
made beds
and faked a smile
for Japanese tourists
who dumped
pockets full of yen
as tips for me

On my day off
boss sister

asked me to clean
our moldy shower
I moved out
into the arms
of my boyfriend
He had a better plan

Move in with me
I will charm you the rest of your days

MOTHER OF ME

If I were the mother of *me*
I wouldn't let me
dress this skimpy
Favorite yellow
halter top, jean shorts
frizzy hair tied back

Lined up against Mike's truck
JR's band and the girls
along for the ride
around the island

Visiting the village saints
showing off
for the new guitar player
By then, Mother lived
on the mainland
and anyway

She knew better

A Party in Agat

1976
Supertyphoon Pamela
tequilla shots and San Miguel Beer

Our beachside home
is common
concrete
bunker-like
built to withstand storms

I am not

We slug drinks
in shuttered rooms
gawk through
our unguarded door
gray with a mad wind

Pamela is merciless
the ocean is coming for us
rain pummeling
I am afraid
reduced to a mop
wringing my hands

The bathroom toilet
a whirlpool
flushing itself

Pamela groans
electricity pops
Gathering round the radio
rallies us in the dark

Oh lovely tropic ranch
mango papaya banana
plumeria and bougainvillea
my typhoon paradise

This is no party
Guam is a mess

He Taught Me How

Sailing was my father's
cure for island fever

Hug the tiller tight
he'd say
watch the boom
as we turn about

My father was a great joker
know why it's called a boom?
because when it hits your head
BOOM

All day we'd sail
till the sea flattened to glass
and the sun setting on the horizon
winked green

Do you see the green flash
my father would ask
as if our sailing bliss
depended upon my answer

Yes I see
I still do

Acknowledgements

My sincere thanks goes to my writing group, Patsy Ann Taylor, Amber Lea Starfire, and Christina Julian, for their patience and skill in critiquing my work. A special thank you to Amber Lea Starfire for formatting and publishing guidance.

For my friends and family, thank you for your encouragement and support, especially my husband, David, for your empathetic ear.

Thank you, too, Elaine Lewis for the generous gift of an original painting for my cover art.

About the Author

Barbara Toboni studied at the University of Guam, earned a certificate at the International Business College of Guam, and holds a Social Sciences degree with Phi Theta Kappa honors from Napa Valley College. Born in Pennsylvania, she lived in Southern California until age thirteen, when her family moved to Guam.  She now lives in Napa, California with her husband. They have two sons.

Undertow, a collection of poetry was published in 2011. Her poetry and short stories have also appeared in newspapers, print and online literary journals, and anthologies, including *Wisdom Has a Voice, Vintage Voices 2011, Cup of Comfort for Parents of Children with Autism,* and *Tiny Lights.*

Ms. Toboni is an active member of the California Writers Club-Santa Rosa and Napa. In 2012, she served as the Redwood Writers Poetry Contest Chair for "Poetry Night." For CWC-Napa, she helps to organize public readings.

barbarasmirror.com

www.ingramcontent.com/pod-product-compliance
Lightning Source LLC
Chambersburg PA
CBHW030311030426
42337CB00012B/677